D0013748

08-AUF-665

KARATE
the art of empty self

TERRENCE WEBSTER-DOYLE

Distributed by
North Atlantic Books
Berkeley, California

Published by
Martial Arts for Peace Association
Middlebury, Vermont

Martial Arts for Peace Association
Atrium Society
P.O. Box 816
Middlebury, Vermont 05753, U.S.A.

Cover Design: Charlene Koonce

Publishers Cataloging-in-Publication

Webster-Doyle, Terrence, 1940-
    Karate : the art of empty self

        1. Karate--Philosophy. 2. Self-knowledge, Theory of. 3. Self-
    defense--Psychological aspects. I Title.
    GV1114.3.W43   1989   796.8153

    ISBN: 0-942941-04-7

Atrium Education For Peace publications are available at discount
for bulk purchases or educational use. Please contact Special Sales
Director, Atrium Society, (800) 848-6021.

Introduction: The Paradox

> Whenever you cross swords with an enemy you must not think of cutting him either strongly or weakly, just think of cutting and killing him. Be intent solely upon killing the enemy.
>
> Miyamoto Musashi,
> a 15th-Century Samurai
> *A Book of Five Rings*

> To subdue the enemy without fighting is the highest skill.
>
> Gichin Funakoshi,
> father of modern Karate
> *Karate-dō—My Way of Life*

There is a fundamental and dangerously different perspective contained in the above quotes; they are two contrasting ways of dealing with conflict; they are also the basis of two radically different approaches to the Martial Arts. One approach lays the foundation for violence and increased aggression under the guise of self-improvement, while the other nurtures self-understanding and intelligence.

The Martial Arts have been portrayed as deadly systems of self-defense techniques. We read of Musashi, the "Sword Saint," who at the early age of 13 killed a person, and went on killing over 60 people before his 30th birthday just to prove that he was invincible. We read other bizarre tales of incredible feats of prowess and strength by Martial Arts "Masters," such as the story of a well-known Karate teacher who killed bulls with his bare hands to prove how strong his method was. Many people want that power, that energy that seems to emanate from one who knows these fighting arts.

There is a great sense of powerlessness today. People are seeking more and more ways to get power, and the Martial Arts, especially Karate, appeals to many. With its emphasis on aggressive fighting skills, and the fascination of mysterious knowledge from the East, it has become increasingly popular. And there are many Martial Arts magazines, schools and instructors who exploit this desire for power and for the arcane.

It seems to me that the traditional *Martial* Arts, the violent, military, egotistic, popularized, romantic view, is a devastatingly perverted misapplication of what is in essence a way of life devoted to developing sensitivity and understanding. Whereas many traditional Martial Arts are concerned primarily with lethal self-defense techniques, conquering and "killing the enemy," and proving one's self through competition, the *Art* of Karate is concerned with understanding violence, "subduing the enemy without fighting," thereby creating the means of going beyond conflict.

The word *Budo* is a key word in the Martial Arts. It means literally, "the way to stop the sword." It also means "the way to stop conflict." The word *Karate* has come to mean "empty hands," to defend oneself without the use of weapons. Its deeper and more significant meaning from a Taoist and Zen Buddhist perspective means "empty self," with the emphasis on *Kara* or "empty." Budo and the Art of Karate as a way to empty self are very similar. The similarity lies in the words *conflict* and *self*. In Karate, as in most Martial Arts practiced worldwide, the self, the ego, the "me" has been glorified, and becomes powerful, dominating, undefeatable, invincible. Traditional Karate uses fighting skills to develop this invincibility, thus creating a steely veneer, a calloused spirit of invulnerability. Lip service is occasionally paid to "spirituality," but actually most practices are really ways to fill one's self up, to inflate and toughen the ego under the guise of self-transcendence. Self-improvement is thus seen as self-enhancement, that is, self-centeredness, focusing inwardly on an image of self that is the root of conflict.

In the Art of Karate we find something radically different. Although one may not see a difference on the surface, it is there. The main similarity of traditional Karate to the Art of Karate is in technique. Both train vigorously in self-defense skills. Both derive confidence from these skills. But this is where the similarity stops and the radical divergence begins. Where traditional Karate begins and ends with technique, the Art of Karate has just begun. The confidence gained in traditional Karate comes from developing technique. The confidence gained in the Art of Karate also comes from technique, but it goes far beyond these skills; its intent is to develop an atmosphere of trust, of understanding. Without this much deeper and more comprehensive aspect of genuine self-enquiry, learning only self-defense skills causes one's practice or understanding to become unbalanced, destructive. Within the context of authentic self-understanding, self-defense skills may have a place, but if one's mistaken goal is to empower the dissociated self, the ego, then one is simply reinforcing fear, which compounds the problem of aggression and violence from isolated self-centered activity.

The Art of Karate is not a *strategy*, "skilled management in getting the better of an adversary," as the word is commonly understood in many traditional forms of the Martial Arts; nor is it a "skillful means of attaining an end." That way is the way of fear, of a cunning mind that is mischievous and detrimental. It is the seed of exploitative "cutthroat" competition; it pits person against person in a struggle for dominance. The Art of Karate is a "non-strategy"—neither a way to get the better of anyone, nor a means to any end that the contrivance of self can create. It is rather a vehicle through which one can understand or have continuous insight into the causes of the breakdown of relationship, thereby bringing about simultaneously a sense of order, harmony and unity.

The intent of the Art of Karate is to give one the opportunity to discover who one is. The intent of the Art of Karate is to act as a mirror so that one can readily and non-judgmentally come into direct relationship with what is usually hidden and resisted. By creating a confident and trusting environment, it allows students to become aware of their pent-up aggressions, tensions and conflicts. Allowing everything that was hidden or resisted to be observed is the central most important aspect in the process of "emptying self"; that is the heart of the Art of Karate. Where the traditional martial approach in Karate develops the tough hide of invulnerability, the Art of Karate fosters flexibility, suppleness and sensitivity. It allows one to be vulnerable—and, paradoxically, this is a great strength. Real power comes from being open, questioning, being susceptible to oneself and others. Only a false sense of power can come from feigning the image of confidence, the image of strength.

If the mind is like still water and reflects what is there without judgment, without distortion, without holding on to what it sees, without saying that what it sees should be anything else, then there is a living moment of learning; then the mind will not fill up with dogmatic assertions, conclusions, opinions. The mind will continually empty itself each moment, renewing itself because it has understood what is reflected and has gone beyond. The water flows, clear and deep, ever new—the mind flows, clear and deep, ever new . . .

> The gift of living
> is to see
> one is an empty vessel
> lost and unknowing.
> Oh—there is love."
> —from *The Wayside*

Foreword

This book is for anyone seriously interested in understanding themselves. One doesn't have to practice the physical aspect of the Art of Karate to benefit from this book. The Art of Karate is simply a context for bringing attention to that which we call our *selves*. This context creates a framework by which one can readily explore the self in action. This exploration is not limited to the practice of Karate. Even outside the Dojo (the place for Karate practice), and without any Martial Arts terminology, the message's universality may be seen by the layperson. All people share these fundamental issues; they are human concerns, of fear and violence. This book addresses these basic concerns, and aims to end them. Through the Art of Karate, the author intends to shed light on what creates and sustains fear and the violence fear begets. The author uses the Art of Karate because he feels that it is an excellent means of allowing one to explore fear openly and nondefensively.

Whether you practice the Art of Karate or any other Martial Art or are a serious layperson, this book will expose you to what is called *empty self.* If you are a practitioner of a Martial Art, this book may help you to lay a foundation for self-understanding intelligently.

In this exploration of empty self, it is vital not to claim that what is written here is the only correct way. These words are offered with great caution, to be shared as a working hypothesis, or as insights that perhaps can be taken as starting points for one's own enquiry.

Throughout the past twenty-five years, the author has observed Karate. At first he thought it to be an effective self-defense. The motivation for it was fear, and, on the surface, Karate seemed to be the answer. As the author practiced and looked deeply and went beneath the surface, he found that the Art of Karate pointed beyond the need to defend oneself. It showed him the conflict inherent in self-defense itself, and the fear underlying this need for self-defense. What he began to see was that the Art of Karate was not a self-defense method, but rather a condition in which one could come to see oneself.

This book offers a collection of insights in self-understanding. They are not conclusions. At best they may stimulate curiosity, interest in understanding oneself, the fear that *is* the self. There is a danger that one may take the word for the thing, which is what we have been educated to do. The word is not the thing, the written insight is not the actual observation. All one can do is to look for oneself, to actually observe oneself without drawing any conclusion. Just to watch. Then there is no assertion, no authority, no body of knowledge that becomes important in itself. One sees, one shares through words what is seen, another hears the words and looks to see if what is being said is true. The seeing is important, not the ideas about seeing. Therefore learning is always direct, immediate. It is never taken over into the next moment as a conclusion, for the next moment is new and must be looked at afresh. There is nothing to accumulate, nothing to fill one's mind with.

This process of direct perception, or continuous nonaccumulative observation, is the essence of empty self. It is always at the beginning. It is not an end point. Therefore, look through the words to see if what is being shared is actually true. Then perhaps these shared insights can awaken a deeper perception of that self that is all mankind.

KARATE
the art of empty self

It is impossible to attack emptiness or to attack from nothingness.

If practiced rightly, the bow expresses, without intention, the essence of the Art of Karate. A mind that has no resistance to life, to what it receives, shows itself in the bow, not by some ritual or conditioned custom but naturally, simply.

The *yoi* or ready stance is the most important stance in the Art of Karate. In this stance, one is alert, aware, attentive. A space is created in this attention, a space where one is not in reaction psychologically, so there is no fear. It seems that fear is present only when one is inattentive.

The Art of Karate aids us in understanding aggression, understanding violence. Too often, violence has been portrayed as a heroic cultural ideal, one that upholds fighting as the honorable solution to conflict. Paradoxically, one can transform hostile aggression by means of Karate. By teaching self-defense skills to the student, one gives him or her the confidence not to fight.

Take Nami Do literally means bamboo, wave, way. It is a metaphor of the relationship between these elements. The bamboo bends, is flexible. In the face of strong forces it yields but does not succumb. This is because it does not resist the force and so by not resisting, it is strong. The wave, in turn, uses its great force to overpower whatever stands in its way, and by sheer brute force is also powerful. Psychologically, the bamboo means to yield, to not resist inwardly. If one insults you, that insult is listened to, understood, and gone beyond. There is no need to react to the insult. Therefore one is free, beyond the conflict of reaction. Psychologically, the wave represents that insult, that anger, that need to hurt another. Physically, the bamboo is the block, the wave is the strike, punch or kick. In order to bring about an intelligent practice one must have the right relationship between these elements, to create a way that is balanced, whole.

It is only by really listening, seeing, that we can understand the truth or falseness of something. If we listen or observe with care, we will be able to find out what is below the surface of things, that which is ordinarily hidden when we only hear or look. In our practice it is important to listen, to observe, to take that quality of attention with us when we leave the dojo to go about our daily lives. For the Art of Karate is life, it is not separate from it.

One cannot create the Art of Karate by practice or by any means contrived by thought. It seems that when there is order in one's life, then that allows the Art to happen. This Art is beyond one's practice, for it is the Art of living.

In Karate we can attack or be attacked. In being attacked we can wait for the other person's initiative, and then respond by evading the attack. These actions are in the realm of reaction. What is needed is an awareness of the potential for attack before it manifests itself in the consciousness of the other person, before the other person is aware of it in themselves. By being highly sensitive to the potential for aggression, we can prevent that potential from ever coming into awareness. This is the ultimate art of reconciliation, for there is no division between people from the beginning.

It is vitally important in our practice of Karate to give ourselves totally, with no holding back. Usually, we don't do this. We resist on some level, and therefore we lack real spirit. When we can give ourselves totally, then we burn away the fear that holds us back. We have tremendous energy when we are fully committed. Fear comes when we remember something in the past, thereby creating a division in the present. When we give ourselves totally, then the past with all its fears is burned away in the flame of that total movement.

Being really free, not only in theory but actually, not only in practice but in our everyday life, is the real meaning of the Art of Karate.

The fear created in thought can transfer to the body, showing up in fixed positions of fear/defense. Take, for example, the defensive rigid posture of the neck pulled back or jutting chin ("take it on the chin"). It seems that the body gets stuck in a flight-or-fight dilemma, and isn't able to move in either direction. One needs to free the body from its fixed postures. This can be done through rigorous workouts, going through a great many simulated fight-or-flight situations. Through this mock battling, one can also begin to unlock the fixed patterns of behavior associated with the fixed bodily patterns. Freeing up the patterns has a healthy effect, because the person can operate in the present without the neurosis of the past. Freed from the past, the body becomes intelligent, active, alive.

The correct execution of a proper technique in all its many facets, both psychological and physical, takes many years of rigorous training to accomplish, and yet, paradoxically, it takes no time at all. It is the expression of the purest and most natural form of one's innate grace and harmony. When properly executed, a technique becomes the expression of unselfconscious skill in action, the Artfulness in the Art of Karate. The outcome of this skill is to transform the person. This transformation takes the person out of time and the self as we know it, and hence out of the conflict and violence of becoming, and creates a still point where there is only the essence of pure action.

If we come to the Art of Karate hoping to learn a self-defense, we will end up in the same state of mind we started out with, but much more seriously compounded. For if we want to learn a self-defense, our state of mind is fear. In the more traditional Karate schools, this fear never gets addressed, except in a superficial way by learning how to fight. This only covers up the fear temporarily. It is the fear at the core of our desires that has to be addressed directly and not covered over by moving away from it through learning how to defend oneself.

The Art of Karate is an integrated, holistic practice. It educates the whole person, the mind/body. Therefore, it is important to spend time on the mind/body, not dividing it to concentrate only on the perfection of technique. Our practice should be designed not only to train in perfecting the physical aspects, the elements of self-defense, but, simultaneously, we need to understand the psychological principles. As we give a great deal of energy to learn the fundamentals of self-defense, we need to work very hard in understanding the reasons for self-defense, why we study Karate and how it can aid in the understanding of ourselves.

Our progression in the Art of Karate is based
metaphorically on the four seasons. The beginner is
like the tender young flower blooming in the Spring;
the student is earnest and energetic, bursting forth
with much energy. As the student moves along, his
or her form becomes like the fire of Summer, the
heat generated by form well-practiced. Then, as the
student ages, a wisdom can come that happens after
the stages of development where the student is
tempered by the duration of intense practice. This is
like the Fall, with seasonal aging. This wisdom
deepens like the whitened drifts of Winter and
finally, like an animal climbing a tree to protect
itself from the cold, it leaves no trace of itself in the
newly falling snow.

The movements in the Art of Karate are at first a
form of controlled free expression. This can have
the effect of venting stored aggressions and freeing
the body to move without the restrictions placed on
it by fear. But as one goes deeper, there is
expression that is not controlled. It is this
movement that is truly free.

The Art of Karate is not a means of self-expression. It is an opportunity for self-understanding, of going beyond one's self.

When we are confronted by a challenge, by someone threatening us, we usually react to the situation. *Reaction*, as it is used here, is a psychological movement to defend, either physically or with words, that which is perceived as being threatened—which is ourselves. It is easy to understand defending oneself from physical assault, but psychological assault is another type of threat. In being attacked physically, the body is being threatened. In being attacked psychologically, what is threatened? If we could actually be aware psychologically at the moment of attack, we could see what is defending. Isn't it our self, an image that thought has created? It seems that the real work of the Art of Karate is in understanding this "self," for it seems that this self is the root of psychological reaction, and therefore is the seat of conflict.

What action can bring about the end of the
psychological self? Our usual approach is to try to
end it through thinking, which is the logical process
of analysis. But if the self has been brought into
being through thought, can thought end it? It seems
that thought can produce only more of itself, and
therefore is not the action to end itself. It seems
that the action to end the psychological reaction is
space, that is, inaction. This seems paradoxical
because our usual idea of action is a movement
generated by thought. But we have seen that
thought is not the answer, so therefore inaction,
which is not the interference of thought, creates a
space in the process of reaction. This space, as
exemplified in the ready stance, is not action as we
are used to. It is rather a watching, actually, in the
moment, staying with the sensation of the
psychological reaction. In this there is no movement
away from the challenge or reaction. There is an
intention to find out through observation what is
going on. That is all. The real challenge is now to
do it.

The main intention of the Art of Karate is love.
Being concerned with love is being concerned that
the students are kind and genuinely affectionate.
Love is not some sentimental emotion, but is
intelligence, understanding, which brings
compassion. It is helping the young students see the
importance of order, of bringing about sensitivity in
their lives. We start our practice by ordering our
shoes by the entrace of our dojo. This could become
a mechanical routine and even take on some
"religious" significance if allowed. But being keenly
aware of the mind's need to do this, a space is
created where this tendency does not enter. So, love
is the essence, the heart of Karate, because it is
alive, active, intelligent, it is constantly awake,
observing the reactions of a mind surrounded by
fear. Then the mind is emptying, not filling up with
ignorant attitudes or blind assumptions about life.

Many people come to Karate with the notion that it will help them. Many people, therefore, look on Karate as a sort of religion, as a way to transcend their problems. This is false right at the beginning. What has to be seen is one's original intention. Rarely does a person do this. Rather, they avoid confronting themselves, burying their intentions in the results they are trying to attain. This only creates more problems and leads one to seek for more help.

One needs an atmosphere of affection and understanding where one practices Karate. Too often, the atmosphere is fear and ignorance.

Karate brings attention to violence. In everyday life, we deny our violence or try to act non-violently by suppressing it in favor of some glorified ideal. It seems important to allow ourselves the opportunity to come into direct contact with all of who we are.

It is important to come into direct contact with our violence, to not cover it up with idealistic behavior. The Art of Karate allows us the opportunity to do just this by creating an environment of trust. The word *trust* here means that nothing is hidden. Also, one needs a controlled environment, with precise limits set on one's behavior in their practice. This controlled environment of trust allows us to act without unnecessary internal restraints, and without giving license to our violence. There is a "middle way," in which we don't move between the polar extremes of repression and expression. In this nonmovement there is intelligence, which is understanding the violence and going beyond it.

All ideals create their opposite. There is a saying in Latin: "Demon est Deus Invertus," which means the Devil is God inverted. When the mind invents an ideal, such as creating a God, then that brings conflict between the ideal and the actual. If the mind is trying to rid itself of what it perceives as bad, either inside oneself or in the world, by setting up ideals for one to follow, then that unintelligent act will produce the opposite of what it intends through the destructive tension this creates through conformity.

It is intelligent to come into direct contact with the actual, the fact without any ideal, without the illusion of the should. In direct contact there is no conflict, there is only the actual, such as violence, which is fear and resistance. So, to set up an ideal in order to change behavior only brings more misery. Many people expect the Martial Arts to be a way out of their problems, and it may be. But the process of setting up the Martial Art as an ideal or set of standards and rules to be followed, causes the problem, the conflict. This same process occurs in religion—and to some people that's what a Martial Art is. This is destructive both to the student and to the teacher, for in this there is no real learning, that is, understanding oneself from moment to moment, looking afresh at what one encounters as life unfolds. All a Martial Art like Take Nami Do can do for people, besides teaching them defense skills, is to mirror who they really are without illusion, to bring student and teacher face to face with themselves. If there is any movement away from this direct contact, then the mind, thought, has created the conflict, the division between the fact and the need to overcome the fact. The seeming paradox is that one changes by not trying to change, for the effort of trying is the effort of idealistic behavior, and the seed of divisive, fragmented action. So, we have to be very careful and alert when we train in the Martial Arts, to see what we are doing, why we are training, what we want out of it and how we are going about getting it. For we could very well be promoting more violence in the name of peace.

We practice with full power because it allows us to go beyond ourselves. In going beyond ourselves we are beyond fear, therefore we are free.

There is a formula in Karate: Attitude and form equal speed, which in turn equals power. Most people want power in the beginning, forgetting that this is a developmental process. If one has an intelligent attitude and practices form only, one's movements will naturally become more rapid and hence more powerful. But one must stay always with attitude and form.

True respect is the essence of the Art of Karate. Respect is the right relationship between teacher and student and between student and student. Respect comes from real affection and not from meaningless rote tradition. It is not following some code of ethics set down by another. Respect then becomes repetition, blind allegiance. Respect is alive, active. It is not the dead weight of the past, no matter how glorified the past may seem to be.

Many students feel the need to prove themselves in Karate. This can be seen in the attainment of better and better form or being the best in the competitive aspect of fighting. Or this will manifest itself in the attainment of rank for prestige. This need to prove oneself can be very obvious or very subtle. Either way it is the same. Perhaps one thinks that by proving oneself, he or she will gain favor or respect. One is therefore caught endlessly satisfying the need for approval, and, in so doing, destroys true respect. In Karate, how well you perform is not important. Excellence in form doesn't come from technical proficiency alone. It comes from an inner quality of affection and sensitivity. It comes from the lack of the need to prove oneself.

It is important to have well-defined form and tradition in Karate, for this allows one to feel safe to explore the depths of violence in oneself because the environment is controlled, limited.

There is a step-by-step process of development in Karate, if one is to attain skill in the physical aspects, the movement of power expressed in the Karate forms. At the foundation is what is called basics, the simple repetitious practice of a block, punch, kick or strike. This foundation is built upon by the combination of two or more basic movements. These combinations are further elaborated upon when they become formalized in forms called Katas. Too often, as a student progresses in the perfection of technique, he or she becomes bored with the basics and wants to move past form to the study of weapons or the like, forgetting the essence of practice. But if we are truly studying the Art then we must adopt the attitude of always being a beginner, of being able to do the basics anew each time. This is difficult, not because it takes effort but rather because it doesn't. What is difficult is the urge to do more, to accomplish for the sake of accomplishment. We need to understand the boredom, the restlessness in oneself, this need to fill oneself up.

When we practice the prearranged movements of the Art of Karate in the Kata, what is our motive, our reason for doing them? Is it for self-expression, or to learn how to defend ourselves better? Why do we have a motive, what purpose does it serve? Is it necessary to be motivated? Or can we practice out of the form itself? This means letting the impulse move us. The impulse is not a motive. It comes on its own and not through the wishes we have to be better or more powerful. Therefore, it is free of any limitations of thought, of the past. Therefore, our movements take on a quality of creativity, of being outside time and then outside the form itself.

One is divided psychologically into two opposing or warring camps. It is the struggle between good and evil. One can see this in Karate, where one is battling against the opponent, the opponent really being oneself. One feels deeply that one must defeat the opponent, win over the enemy. Traditional Karate perpetuates this division, this battle, this contest, by its emphasis on fighting skills. This only breeds fear, not understanding.

Gichin Funakoshi, the father of Karate-do, stated,
"To subdue the enemy without fighting is the
highest skill." What is the meaning of *subdue*? Who
is the enemy? And how is one fighting the enemy?
To subdue means to overpower by superior force, to
conquer, vanquish, oppress. Another meaning is to
put at rest, quiet, soothe, calm, still. Here are two
different meanings. One is forceful, controlling. The
other controls in a more peaceful manner, with
ease, with gentleness. Yet both are strong in dealing
with the enemy. And who is this enemy? It may
seem that the enemy is another, as in war. But here,
perhaps, the enemy is one's self, the internal battle
of thought trying to control itself. Fighting, then, is
not done with weapons or with the body but with
the mind, for the mind is divided and is in a state of
conflict, producing outside itself a world of conflict
and violence. So can the "highest skill" be to put to
rest, to quiet or still the internal "enemy" created by
the divided self, a self at war with itself? How does
one find out about this, to see if there is truth in
this? Perhaps this is the "highest skill," that is,
finding out the truth or falseness of something.
Could this process be called intelligence, this
capacity to understand through direct observation
the truth about one's state of mind, a mind that has
created this violent and fearful world?

The Art of Karate as an Art of self-defense is an
ethical approach to the resolution of conflict,
because it is a discipline that develops the
confidence to neutralize hostility by alternative,
non-violent means.

The Art of Karate, when done with affection, with beauty of movement, gives dignity and grace to the body, which in turn gives great dignity and grace to the spirit. One's movements have symmetry and there is elegance in their flowing design. This refinement in the way one moves has an effect on one's relationship with another, bringing to it a sense of ease and charm. One naturally wants to bring symmetry to one's life, having manners, being polite, gracious, kind. This is not contrived. It is authentic, arising out of a genuine impulse for order and intelligence.

The word *Dojo* means a training hall or gymnasium where the Japanese Martial Arts are practiced. Its more literal translation means, "the place of the way," or "a place of awakening." When one practices Karate within the Dojo, it defines a space where one's form is contained and nurtured. This limitation of space gives limits to one's activity, and thereby brings freedom in that limitation. Having a definition gives one the opportunity to explore, it gives one the opportunity to be observant of that movement. Exploring is awakening, it is insight into the way things are, for life has its limitations, its order is according to the laws of nature. When one sees this, there is conformity in harmony with the way of things. When one enters the Dojo, one can sense the order, the natural conformity with the way things are. This is not resignation, nor is it conformity that is blind, that one follows without question. The Dojo must reflect the natural order, and, in so doing, free the student.

Focus in Karate is when one concentrates one's total energy at one point. At first this is done intentionally, because the student is beginning to learn technique. Focus, when practiced over a long period, should go beyond technique. It should happen of itself without intention. Focus is then spontaneous and natural. It is as natural part of a person as is walking or sitting. It is not something one has to try to do. But what often happens is that the advanced student still goes on trying to perfect focus, to make his or her form more powerful. This happens when focus becomes the aim of self-expression, or a means of gaining something through the perfection of technique. Genuine focus has no motive, and therefore creates affection.

Put the thought of achieving right out of your mind. Give your full attention to form and move from there. In this you will never be bored. Even the student of many years still practices the basics as if for the first time. This has been called beginner's mind, a mind that is fresh, renewed each moment.

Kata is form. It is a set of prearranged movements, a
routine one practices in order to become proficient
in the self-defense aspect of Karate. In this way,
Kata is a set or customary order of doing something,
it is a structure or pattern one follows to attain a
result. Kata as form is, therefore, a formality
moulded by instruction and discipline. Yet form
moves beyond defense, beyond result and formality.
When one first practices Kata it is mechanical, as is
necessary in order to learn technique properly. After
practicing Kata for a time, one brings forth spirit,
the energy generated from contacting the essence of
the Kata, that movement that is not of time. The
beauty of the movement is then for itself alone. In
form with spirit there is dignity and gracefulness in
the gesture. There is a majestic quality to
movement when one's spirit is complete. In this,
one gives one's total attention to that form, to live
in the world with one's own body, here and now.
Then, form and kata are one and the same, and that
form is in everything one does. Kata becomes
complete action and the form pervades all activity.
Kata becomes ethics, it becomes conduct, it is how
one behaves. It is the intention towards right
behavior. Form as Kata puts that which is, in order.
It gives shape and order to how one acts in the
world.

We may find that when we are challenged or threatened from without, we go into what psychologists call a "fight-or-flight" reaction. This means that we react to the situation by recoiling into a defensive position or running away, or by attacking. This reaction to external threat is sometimes necessary for survival, as when we need to avoid a car coming at us or to defend ourselves from assault. But this reaction is inappropriate when we react to supposed threats from within, and the fight-or-flight reaction is triggered when we feel endangered psychologically.

There are stories of "Zen Masters" hitting their students on the head with sticks when the students asked them questions about a state beyond their confusion, a state called enlightenment. If we ask about our lives, if we seek solutions in our turmoil, is it that we do not know the answer, and therefore if we find an answer we will solve our problems? Do our lives have answers, solutions? Isn't seeking answers to the whys of life asking the unanswerable? Doesn't this create only more confusion? When the mind is confused, looking for answers either maintains confusion or resists it by trying to end it. Either way perpetuates and compounds confusion by adding the additional conflict of being at odds with our confusion. Confusion is confusion. Just eat, sleep and let the mind sort itself out. Like muddy water, the mud settles when left alone.

The problem that causes self-protective or defensive aggressive reactions is fear. Our traditional approach to this problem says that aggression is the honorable way to deal with fear and the conflict it produces, whether on the individual, national or international level. Karate, as taught in most schools, has carried on this practice, so that the student is taught primarily how to fight, thereby producing more aggression, which in turn reinforces the fear and defensiveness, in what is called a vicious circle. This approach only compounds the original problem and does not lend understanding toward ending it.

In karate, we see students practicing with great
intensity, using a great deal of energy in their
movements, trying to be powerful. They are forcing
the body, through a series of contractions and
expansions of the muscles, to be strong, to be
skillful in defending themselves. But there seems to
be a contradiction in this process; in order to be
able to act quickly in any given moment, one must
be very flexible, spontaneous. Therefore, one must
not be caught up in the force of the movements, or
become committed to directing one's energy in such
as way as to force the body to become hard,
unyielding. This process, if it is allowed to continue,
develops a hardness of spirit, a rigidity of character.
This hardness too often is mistaken for strength, a
state of mind coveted because it seems powerful.
But this immutability prevents any real flow of life;
it creates a general insensibility and callousness.
One needs a delicacy of movement, a sensitivity to
the fine tuning of the body as it moves in response
to action outside itself. This means that we are
aware of the minute details of our practicing, keenly
observing ourselves in action. This means putting
aside any image of what it means to do Karate or to
be powerful. It means only that we are conscious,
without thinking, of the seemingly infinite reactions
we have. By not trying to be strong, we find that
there is an energy that is not effort, that is not
forced. This energy comes out of the dispassionate
interest of awareness itself, which thereby allows us
to respond to external challenges appropriately

without the hindrance of fear, because fear seems to create the seeds for this effort to become powerful. All this takes an attitude of wanting to really understand what the meaning of *Kara* (empty) in Karate means and the significance this might have upon relationship. For if all we are doing is learning self-defense skills because we are afraid, then we are only perpetuating violence in the world. The Art of Karate is concerned with understanding violence and ending it. In learning about what creates conflict, there is freedom from it.

In one's practice, one may become aware of one's aggression. This observation may lead one to denying that aggression. This can produce in the mind an ideal of non-aggression, an image to become, to emulate. A person who denies aggression for the ideal of non-aggression is, paradoxically by the very act of denial, doing violence to themselves as a result. And when one denies aggression, one denies the real passion, the real energy needed to understand the problem. Or, at the other extreme, one can act out that aggression towards another through competing with him or her in fighting. Both are reactions, and are therefore unintelligent. In the Art of Karate one needs to understand how the mind works, how it creates the extremes, the polarities of reaction. In understanding this, the student does not get caught in either extreme. This is not another form of action but rather inaction, not acting out of reaction. Seeing this, one is free psychologically, one is not in conflict inwardly.

The mind becomes rigid in its conditioned views of the world, seeing life through fear, through self-centered reactive thinking. This rigid thought process affects the body, putting it into postures of defense, into rigid patterns of behavior that affect natural movement. This causes the body to become ill, dis-eased. This affects the whole person in the totality of life. The Art of Karate can help inhibit this debilitating process through its rigorous workouts, in which the body not only releases the tension that holds these rigid holding patterns in place but at the same time touches on the root of the problem, the fear that caused the problem in the first place.

There is nothing mystical about Karate. It is just intelligent, hard work. There are many people who exploit the Art of Karate by promising the student something special, such as enlightenment. This is just another illusion, another image the mind conjures up in its need to substantiate itself, to fill itself up. This leads to self-expression and the need to demonstrate what one has learned. There is no secret about Karate, there is nothing concealed or hidden. It is not supernatural in any way. It has been shrouded in Eastern mysticism, which appeals to the Western mind. The literature about the Martial Arts seems to the Occidental mind arcane, esoteric. This was probably done because they were trying to create a myth for the nation, for the tribe. It is a primitive form of relationship founded on fear. The intelligent mind is moving beyond these superstitious ways of relating to life. So it is important to see that Karate can be new and open, taking what is sensible and necessary for one's practice and leaving the old in the past. One must actually see that Karate is very simple, which is, paradoxically, quite difficult for the overly educated and sophisticated contemporary mind. One just needs to do the basics with great care, observing the mind's reactions. The basics are the Karate movements in the Dojo and the movement of each moment in one's daily life, the commonplace tasks of simple living. When washing dishes, observe; when reading this book, observe. The ordinary phenomena of everyday life are lessons in

themselves, there is nothing beyond them. See the
beauty and freedom in this. The ordinary is then the
extraordinary and is truly mysterious. But this
cannot be sought and captured by any intention, any
way or method that the mind could create. The Art
of Karate is not a way to anything; it can only
create a condition that brings attention to the way
we live, to our attitudes about life. It shows one
their violence, how life is destroyed by conditioned
thinking, which is based on fear.

Empty self and love are in essence the same. This is
not an ideal to conform to, but a reality to
understand. It is not merely a concept, an
intellectual speculation, but an actual fact. It is not
a projection of a frightened mind but an insight into
the nature and structure of ourselves
psychologically. The Art of Karate is an opportunity
where we can begin to bring the insight into reality
by coming into direct contact with unexplored
regions of ourselves.

In helping the students understand the Art of Karate, one points out to them the fundamental causes of fear, defensiveness and aggression, one helps them develop creative nonviolent alternatives to aid in reducing or preventing the reactions caused by fear. In helping the students, one teaches them self-defense skills to give them confidence, so they don't have to fight. It is also important to create a safe and trusting environment, so that students can work through or act out their need for aggression within the Karate form, so that hostile gestures (punching, kicking or striking) can be transformed into an art form, and thus reduce stored tension within the body.

In the process of understanding and learning about violence and aggression through a rigorous training in Karate techniques, a student gains a greater sense of confidence in his or her ability to deal nonviolently with hostile aggression. When a student has gained this sense of confidence, the mind/body is freed from the inhibiting force of fear that is produced by the threat of hostile aggression, thereby creating a clear and fearless mind/body that is able to deal more effectively and successfully with violence in more creative ways. Some examples of creative alternatives could be: walking away, using humor, trickery, agreeing, making friends, screaming and so on—the possibilities may be endless. In other words, a student can learn effective self-defense skills, that is, how to protect him- or herself, so he or she can be confident enough not to fight, and therefore use nonviolent alternatives to transform hostile aggression.

_____

It is our work, if it is serious and genuine, that is important, and not the person.

One may discover the essence of the Art of Karate in any endeavor. If one is sensitive, there is the potential for learning. One may be a gardener, potter, housekeeper, businessman, or teacher—it really makes little difference what one does as long as there is intelligence. The Art of Karate is different only in that it is more direct in its exploration of the reactions of the conditioned mind, in its understanding of empty self.

In Karate we *kiai*, which is a type of yell or shout. This shout does two things. First, the expelling of air through the mouth in a strong, vibrant manner helps give focus to the Karate movement or technique by making it stronger. This happens because the abdominal muscles contract and give extra power. The kiai also has the effect of psychologically disarming a potential assailant; the tremendous energy generated by the kiai can shake the assailant's intention to do you harm, for it temporarily disorients him. It can also reach deeply into the person and make contact in a fundamental way; the kiai can bring the person back to his or her senses, back from the depths of fear and hurt to the clear and untainted moment. This can be a very shocking thing, especially when it occurs suddenly. It is like being doused with cold water when you are asleep. It brings you out of your dream world into the blazing daylight of reality. This sudden awakening from one's nightmare into the moment is the intention of the Art of Karate. Sustaining that state is another matter, and must be approached in a different manner.

Also, *kiai* simply means energy and union, as in Aiki(do). Unifying energy means to bring an end to conflict. When conflict is absent, then naturally there is harmony, which is a state of unified energy. The lack of harmony or discord means a state of fragmented energy, a divided state. When one is intending to act out of fear, hurt and anger, then one is out of harmony with things as they are, for these qualities are born of the mind when there is a state of conflict. Being free of the disorder of fearful thinking, one is undivided, not isolated from living. When one kiais, then one is not only focusing energy for more power or to psychologically disarm an assailant; it has a much more far-reaching effect—it affects the whole balance of nature. So, when you kiai, what are you doing? Where does this energy generate from in you? Is it out of fear, which just adds more conflict? Or is the kiai a mightier shout, as an expression of the union of energy within and without? If the latter is true, then one's actions are always in accordance with nature's harmony, even if you have to defend yourself. There is no conflict in one's actions. There is only the appropriate response to the moment and the great undivided force of energy meeting that response.

In sensing a potential hostile situation, we can, by being non-defensive, open, alert, turn that potential for destruction into something constructive. Most people cannot act appropriately because they are afraid. Therefore, they act defensively out of fear, which in turn begets fear.

There is a point in one's practice where it is still, like the eye of a hurricane. This still point comes when there is no resistance, when there is effortless attention without a center, without someone attending. In that empty space, there is a feeling of limitlessness, but one wouldn't recognize it as such at that moment. It is only afterward, when one recollects that there is this comparison. There is no way one can bring about this stillness. It just happens. Perhaps one can set the stage, so to speak, for this to happen, by being aware, intelligent, by understanding all that the mind does to cloud perception, to fill itself with thoughts of fear. But there cannot be any intention to get that stillness; unfortunately, it is rare and, most often, intention dismisses occurrence. It seems as if the mind dismisses this stillness in favor of the "normal" state of consciousness, that of a constant anxious tension that is called living. The stillness is usually quickly brushed aside, perhaps because the mind is afraid of living without fear, it is too out-of-the-ordinary. But perhaps this stillness is the real, is the actual state of living, and one's normal life is the abnormal.

When we practice the movements in Karate, what are our bodies doing? Many people create a great deal of tension in themselves trying to be more powerful. As they move, their bodies move downward, compacting into rigid habitual patterns of defense. Thus compacted, their bodies become tight, less flexible. Their movements become slower and, therefore, less powerful. Can this tendency to move downward, compacting the movements of the body, be inhibited? When this occurs, there is a natural movement upward, allowing spaces in the body, so that it is more flexible. Then our movements are more effortless, less confining. Our movements are likened to snapping a wet towel, which is loose, but suddenly and effortlessly concentrated at a point of contact, giving a sharp and focused feeling. Movements, therefore, can happen of themselves in an appropriate response to what is there.

In Karate, we hear our instructors speak of manners, of proper behavior or, in other words, etiquette. Hopefully, it is obvious what good manners are, especially in the Dojo. But how does one behave really? Is it because we are told to do so, because it is a part of the rules? Or is there something within ourselves that wants order in relationship, some intrinsic need for proper behavior. For, if there is this internal sense for order, for proper behavior, then there is no need to impose it from the outside, by another, as many do when they are trying to force us to act in accordance with their unintelligent demands.

Karate increases sensitivity, but only if it is seen in perspective. We cannot benefit from Karate if we see it as the whole of life. Karate may have a place in life, but this place must be understood in relation to the rest of living. Many people take Karate and make it everything because they are afraid. They do not understand the relativity of all things. Out of fear, they exploit the self-defense aspect, which is only one small part of the total. In this way, one's understanding becomes unbalanced, distorted. Understanding the relationship of the part to the whole is balance and harmony. Then, our practice of Karate becomes integrated into the rest of our lives in a natural and fluid manner. There is then no separation between Karate and living. Then, paradoxically, the part becomes the whole and the whole the part. We are not divided. But we must be careful not to try to approach the whole, the totality of life through the fragment, through Karate, as though it were the whole.

In the Art of Karate, we are constantly being
confronted by ourselves, our fears, our distrust, our
need to defend, to react from our need to protect
and therefore prove ourselves. We tend to see these
qualities as coming from the outside, from others,
when in fact it is ourselves we are looking at. Our
practice, therefore, becomes a mirror, a direct
perception of who we really are, and not the
idealized image of whom we wish to be. In this
honest, uninhibited observation, there is the
beginning of the understanding of the self, and the
emptying of that.

In Karate, as in life, we think of gain, of how far we have progressed. One of the first questions that a prospective student usually asks is how long it takes to get the Black Belt. In this pursuit, we are concentrated on images in the future. These images are our picture of ourselves and the world we want to live in. This sets up a view of how life should be, and creates conflict between our ideal and the fact of how things actually are. Because of this image of ourselves and the world, we want to control what happens, to have power over our lives and what affects us. The way we try to accomplish this is through developing an attitude of being strong. So, perhaps one way we try to be strong, to control life, is to study a Martial Art. Many people see a Martial Art as a powerful force that will enable the practitioner to bring life in line with their self-centered needs, needs created by our fears of not getting what we want. Therefore, it seems important to see what our intention is when we ask about our progress, our need to measure in terms of gain. We may be asking to see gain in the physical realm, to see a progression in our technique, but this often gets translated into the psychological realm. Gain in the psychological realm only reinforces the self, the need to prove ourselves, which only creates more conflict. The intention of the Art of Karate is to end conflict at its root, psychologically. Too often Karate is being taught unintentionally as a means of perpetuating psychological conflict because it asks the students to look at themselves only superficially. In the traditional forms of Martial Arts, there is a focus on perfecting the physical, the body, in performing more and better technique. Technique has its place but only within a larger context of understanding the whole person, the psychological as well as the physical. If we are concerned only with technique, then we are filling the self up with the arrogance of how good we are, which many people take for confidence. Real confidence comes from an intelligent understanding of the self that is the foundation for the Art of Karate.

Training the body in self-defense to know the right thing to do in a threatening situation is essential in ending conflict. If the body doesn't know how to respond properly to a potentially hostile situation, more fear is created and, therefore, a need to defend psychologically. The body needs to know what to do, so it can create a space in which there is no reaction.

In the Art of Karate, it is important to act without reaction, to act clearly out of what one perceives, out of what is there and not out of what one fears. Therefore, one must be aware of one's motivations, to see that one doesn't have to be a prisoner of thought. Understanding one's motivations, understanding the nature and structure of fear, one does not identify with one's conditioned thinking. The thoughts come, the thoughts go—when one is aware. In this, one is free from conditioned reactions and, therefore, free of the need to react defensively from fear. Then, one is truly a student of the Art of Karate, because one is constantly learning about oneself.

"Empty self" is not another form of nonviolence. Neither is it a license to be violently aggressive. The physical self-defense skills learned in the Art of Karate are not designed to be used in an offensive manner. Yet at times it may be appropriate to stand up to the self-centered aggression of another and, if need be, to use controlled force to counter physical violence. Meeting energy with energy, confronting aggression straight on, may look like violence to those who have been conditioned to act out of some ideal of nonviolence. They may imagine that "empty self" means that one acts passively, "turning the other cheek." But affecting nonviolence denies the energy necessary to meet the arrogance of self-centered aggression. Energy is dissipated when one conforms to images or ideals of nonviolence.

Paradoxically, conforming to ideals of nonviolence is a self-destructive process. A psychological conflict arises between one's real self and one's image of oneself—between the truth of who one actually is and the fantasy, or idealized nonviolent image of who one wants to become. The harder one tries to be nonviolent, the greater the pressure to be what one is not. The paradox is that the very act of trying to be nonviolent generates violence. Action stemming from this inward division is manifested outwardly as conflict in relationships.

Meeting energy with energy, without self-centered motivation, without defending or asserting oneself, may be the only intelligent course of action.

It is important to see that the problem of fear and aggression, the conflict it creates and the inappropriate traditional approach in trying to solve it, is a fundamental cause of violence, not only individually but collectively, not only as disharmony within oneself but as a major breakdown of human relationship. The ensuing strife this situation creates among people is reflected in competition and, ultimately, in war. It is also important to see that this problem must be dealt with, not only at the collective level with law and political reform, but, more importantly, at the individual level from where it arises. Social reform and the law are only temporary measures at best. Understanding these deeper insights lays the right foundation for the practice of Karate as a system of self-defense skills.

When practicing Karate, do not concern yourself with thoughts of self-defense. This has only fear as its motivation. If one is fearful, there is no understanding.

In Karate, we sit quietly before we practice and at the end of the practice. This is called *Mukuso*. We do this so we can have a moment to allow ourselves to become relaxed, calm. Being relaxed, calm we can concentrate fully on what we are doing without distraction. But, more importantly, sitting quietly we have the opportunity to observe our thinking, to see the thoughts that are running constantly through the brain. Becoming aware of thought, we can begin to see the roots of self-centered activity, the fears that form our behavior because thought affects behavior, thought creates behavior. We begin to see how behavior is conditioned by thoughts of fear, mainly fear of self survival. Sitting quietly opens up the depth of our selves. In this, the roots of violence are revealed. We are then understanding the essence of the Art of Karate, we then begin to understand the significance of empty self.

Two young students gave me these simple poems to
read to the other students.

    i am nobody
    a red sinking Autumn sun
    took my name away

    In the falling snow
    a laughing boy holds out his palms
    until they are white

Karate is actually very simple. There is nothing special about it at all. If we could only see this, our practice will be very special indeed!

We ask our young students to put their shoes by the entrance of our place of practice. They line them up just so, taking care to observe the order in this simple gesture. They think that Karate is punching and kicking. We know that the Art of Karate is lining up their shoes—just so.

In the beginning we study the Art of Karate because of a need for power, because we are afraid. If we are intelligent, this stage passes and we find that we study because we want to understand what the deeper meaning is. This is when we come to see that Karate means "empty self," and this is where our practice takes on real significance.

The Martial Arts For Peace Association

The Martial Arts for Peace Association's (MAPA) intention is to understand the source of violence, the nature and structure of conflict within the human mind; develop intelligent, non-violent alternatives to conflict; and create safe and trusting environments, providing people with the opportunity to allow this conflict, and the tension and aggression it creates, to be explored.

Through its Centers in Middlebury, Vermont and Sonoma County, California, and workshops and lecture tours throughout the United States and abroad, MAPA promotes Martial Arts not only to develop confidence through self-defense skills, but also to create an understanding of conflict affecting one's behavior, both individually and globally. Thousands of young people have benefited from this innovative and important education, and have experienced a profoundly practical understanding of themselves and the conflicts they so frequently face in daily life—at home, at school, and in the world at large.

The Atrium Society

The Atrium is a place for learning about the conditioned mind, which has brought us to the state of unparalleled conflict and devastation we experience in the world today.

It is concerned with fundamental issues, preventing both understanding and cooperation in human affairs. Our minds are conditioned by origin of birth, education, and experiences. Atrium Society's intent is to bring the issue of conditioning, and the tremendous conflict conditioning creates, to the forefront of awareness and consideration. Its resources include a comprehensive program of books, video tapes, teacher training workshops, school curriculums, and seminars designed to address the primary causes of conflict.

The Martial Arts For Peace Association and the Atrium Society have no established beliefs or ritualistic function and are not allied with any political organization.

DR. TERRENCE WEBSTER-DOYLE, 6th Dan, is Founder and Chief Instructor of Shuhari Aikikarate Do and Director of the Martial Arts for Peace Association (MAPA)—dedicated to promoting peace through the Martial Arts. He has studied and taught the Martial Arts for over thirty years, has post-graduate degrees in Psychology and Education, and is a credentialed secondary and community college instructor. He earned his Black Belt in the Japanese style of Gensei Ryu Karate from Sensei Numano in 1967. Dr. Webster-Doyle has been inducted into both the International and World Martial Arts Halls of Fame. He has worked in Juvenile Delinquency Prevention, presents workshops in Martial Arts programs worldwide, and has written numerous books for adults and young people on understanding conflict.